Emotions, Church, Money & Stuff

Emotions, Church, Money & Stuff

Jack Crabtree
Kevin Flannagan
Mark Oestreicher
Neil Wilson
Len Woods

David Veerman,
Series Editor

VICTOR BOOKS
A DIVISION OF SCRIPTURE PRESS PUBLICATIONS INC.
USA CANADA ENGLAND

TOPICS AVAILABLE IN FLEX SESSIONS

Friendship, Tough Times & God's Will
Success, Pride & a Sex-Crazed Society
Dating, Identity & Bible Study
Sex, the Future & Prayer

Copyediting: Daryl Lucas
Cover Design: Mardelle Ayres

ISBN: 1-56476-091-X

Printed in the United States of America.

1 2 3 4 5 6 7 8 9 10 Printing/Year 97 96 95 94 93

CONTENTS

About the Authors

The authors of **Flex Sessions** are youth ministry veterans, having written and led, collectively, thousands of meetings for high school and junior high young people. These lessons come out of their experiences and creativity.

JACK CRABTREE
Executive Director
Long Island (New York) Youth for Christ

KEVIN FLANNAGAN
Director
East Alabama Area Youth for Christ

MARK OESTREICHER
Junior High Pastor
Calvary Church of Santa Ana, Santa Ana, California

NEIL WILSON
Pastor
Eureka (Wisconsin) United Methodist Church

LEN WOODS
Pastor to Students
Christ Community Church, Ruston, Louisiana

Flex Sessions are produced in cooperation with the Livingstone Corporation, David R. Veerman, Editor. The authors would like to thank Tim Atkins, Claudia Gerwin, Michael Kendrick, and Daryl Lucas for their assistance during the writing of this book.

HOW TO USE THE FLEX SESSIONS

Actually, the whole point of **Flex Sessions** is that you can use them any way you want! Here are a few options to get you started.

The Topics

- Teach all 12 sessions for a balanced quarter's worth of material.
- Promote each topic as a mini-series during the summer or as a change of pace in your regular program.
- Build a retreat around the four sessions of one topic.

Options within the Sessions

- Use them as they're written for high school students, or follow the adaptations for junior high/middle school kids.
- Follow the material in **bold type** as a guideline for those times when you'll be doing the talking.
- Extend a session with the Additional Idea if you have more time available.
- Replace an activity with one from the Additional Idea if you see one your group would love.
- Use the Active Bonus ideas if your setting permits high-energy activities.

Clip Art

- Make a calendar to post or send home picturing the upcoming sessions.
- Photocopy one illustration onto 3" x 5" cardstock along with the time, place, and a brief description of the meeting, and send as a promotional postcard.
- Make postcards to let absent kids know they're missed—and what they're missing.
- Add clip art to the reproducible charts and handouts in the sessions.
- Brighten your bulletin board with illustrations.
- Novelty printers can make T-shirts, hats, 3-ring binders, and just about anything else you might want to use as attendance incentives, give-aways to visitors, or mementos of retreats, etc.
- Don't forget the reduction/enlargement feature if your photocopier has one.

Whether you teach **Flex Sessions** just as they're written, or pick and choose from the options above, you'll find that **Flex Sessions** give you the resources you need for the flexibility you want.

EMOTIONS

Lost in the Crowd

KEY CONCEPT: Overcoming loneliness

BIBLE PASSAGES: Selected passages

OBJECTIVE: As a result of this meeting, students will understand that loneliness is a universal problem and learn how to deal with it in themselves.

MATERIALS CHECKLIST:

- ☐ Bibles
- ☐ Pencils or pens
- ☐ Paper
- ☐ Self-sticking labels
- ☐ Marker
- ☐ Copies of the "Initial Experience" worksheet
- ☐ Copies of the "Loneliness Busters" cards (Action)

JUNIOR HIGH/MIDDLE SCHOOL ADAPTATION: Loneliness can be devastating for early adolescents. Most of them, however, feel lonely many times during each week because they are trying hard to fit into groups at school and because their friends and classmates can be fickle and cruel. This meeting will work well with junior highers with the following changes: Select key verses and discuss them as a whole group instead of dividing into small groups, keep the Challenge short, and use junior high examples.

STARTER

(15 minutes)

Game: Kick Me . . . I'm Lonely

Before the meeting, preprint on self-sticking labels a variety of instructions about how students should respond and react to one another during the mixer (see below). These might include:

Smile at me	Be extremely friendly to me
Talk with me	Ignore me
Make fun of me	Work with me
Glare at me	Show concern for me
Don't listen to me	Don't look me in the eyes
Look me in the eyes	Freely use the phrase, "you jerk" in conversation with me

As the meeting begins, put a label on each person's back and tell everyone not to attempt to find out what his or her tag says.

When everyone has a label with an instruction on it, have the group begin the following activity. Remind them to relate to each person according to what that person's label says. (For example, students should *run from* the person whose label says "Treat me like a leper.")

Mixer: Initial Experience

Hand out copies of "Initial Experience" and tell students to get the initials of people who can truthfully make the claims listed on the sheet.

After a few minutes, stop and see who got the most initials.

STUDY

(20 minutes)

Discussion

Ask:

- **How many of you think you know what instructions are written on the name tag on your back?** Have them share one-by-one and quiz them as to why and how they came to their conclusions.
- **How difficult was it to treat each person according to his or her label?**

Interview

Bring to the front of the room those students who had more negative experiences during the mixer. Ask them the following questions:

- **How did you feel?** (Awkward, self-conscious, nervous, etc.)
- **If you were constantly treated this way, how would you handle it?**
- **What kids at your school are treated this way on a regular basis? Why?**

Of the group as a whole, ask:

- **What are some words that describe how loneliness feels?**
- **What situations make you feel lonely?**
- **When in your life have you felt the loneliest?**

Transition

Explain that loneliness is a universal condition. Share these famous quotes dealing with loneliness:

- **"It is strange to be known so universally and yet be so lonely." (Albert Einstein)**
- **"I hate humanity. I am allergic to it. I see no one. I don't go out. I am disgusted with everything." (Brigitte Bardot)**
- **"We are born into a world where alienation awaits us." (Ronald Liang)**
- **"All man's history is an endeavor to shatter his loneliness." (Norman Cousins)**
- **"Loneliness affects some people all the time and all people some of the time." (Kevin Flannagan)**
- **"Loneliness is the greatest problem facing humanity today." (Billy Graham)**

Small Groups

Break into small groups and look up the following verses. After a few minutes, have each group report what caused each biblical person's lonliness.

- Psalm 31:11-12 (David's loneliness—everyone scorning him)
- 2 Timothy 4:16 (Paul's loneliness—abandoned by friends)
- Matthew 26:69-75 (Peter's loneliness—he abandoned his friend)
- Luke 22:39-46 (Jesus' loneliness—separated from the Father)
- Psalm 66:18 (Our loneliness—sin)

Explain that in God's eyes each person is valuable, important, and never alone. Then give each small group the following references. Have them look them up and report what the passage says about lonliness.

- Isaiah 49:15-16 (God will not forget you.)
- Hebrews 13:5 (God will not leave you.)
- Matthew 28:20 (Jesus promises to be with you.)
- Romans 8:38-39 (Nothing can separate you from God.)
- Joshua 1:9 (God is with you wherever you go.)

CHALLENGE

(3 minutes)

Say something like: **In the Bible study we learned that everyone faces loneliness. But we also discovered that even though loneliness is going to strike, we can be confident that if we turn to Christ and walk with Him, we need never be alone.**

If research is correct, most of us are currently, or will very shortly, be lonely.

Paul Tournier, a famous psychologist and writer, tells of a woman who lived in a large apartment house and worked in a shop with many people. Even though she knew a lot of people, every evening she would tune into the "sign off" statement of a radio station just to hear a voice saying, "We wish you a very pleasant good-night." She imagined that the person was speaking just to her. She hungered for a personal greeting even though she heard scores of people every day. You want a ministry; why not find a lonely person who has no one to say good-night to, and give that person a call each evening? Your night will be far more pleasant for having wished good-night to someone else.

ACTION

(7 minutes)

Assignment

Pass out the Loneliness Busters as wallet-sized cards for kids to keep handy so they will be reminded of what to do when loneliness strikes. Photocopy the worksheet and cut out as many as you need.

Prayer

Have two or three students close in prayer. If possible, end the meeting early and go somewhere as a group for ice cream or frozen yogurt.

ACTIVE BONUS

Reach Out and Tag Someone

Explain that this game is played like tag, except that instead of just touching another person, you need to hug him or her. Also, once a person is hugged, both people are then "it" and must find others to hug. The game ends when everyone has been engulfed in a large group hug. Choose an outgoing, friendly person to be "it" and let the game begin. If you have time, repeat with a new beginning person.

If you feel that your group will be uncomfortable with hugs, have them pat the person on the back.

ADDITIONAL IDEAS

Lonely Look

Before the meeting, cut out a number of pictures from magazines that feature a variety of people in various poses and situations. For example, you could feature a famous athlete, someone modeling the latest fashions, a movie star, a politician, someone in the news, etc. Be sure to include pictures of normal-looking kids. Display the pictures one at a time. Ask the group to identify those whom they think might be lonely. Then discuss what might make those people lonely.

Initial Experience

1. I enjoy eating frog legs.

2. I have been to the Eiffel Tower.

3. I have never had a cavity.

4. I enjoy playing/watching soccer.

5. I have never changed a flat tire.

6. I am available for a dating relationship.

7. I have been on the radio.

8. I have $20 or more in my wallet.

9. I bite my fingernails.

10. I hate cats.

Loneliness Busters

Loneliness Busters

1. Organize a series of games for the children in your neighborhood.
2. Visit a convalescent home or retirement community and talk with some of the residents.
3. Put together a care package for a missionary overseas whom your church supports.
4. Call a friend and work together on a school or youth group project.
5. Run an errand for a neighbor.
6. Volunteer to help out at an inner-city mission or homeless shelter.
7. Help a classmate in a subject in which you excel.

Loneliness Busters

1. Organize a series of games for the children in your neighborhood.
2. Visit a convalescent home or retirement community and talk with some of the residents.
3. Put together a care package for a missionary overseas whom your church supports.
4. Call a friend and work together on a school or youth group project.
5. Run an errand for a neighbor.
6. Volunteer to help out at an inner-city mission or homeless shelter.
7. Help a classmate in a subject in which you excel.

Loneliness Busters

1. Organize a series of games for the children in your neighborhood.
2. Visit a convalescent home or retirement community and talk with some of the residents.
3. Put together a care package for a missionary overseas whom your church supports.
4. Call a friend and work together on a school or youth group project.
5. Run an errand for a neighbor.
6. Volunteer to help out at an inner-city mission or homeless shelter.
7. Help a classmate in a subject in which you excel.

Loneliness Busters

1. Organize a series of games for the children in your neighborhood.
2. Visit a convalescent home or retirement community and talk with some of the residents.
3. Put together a care package for a missionary overseas whom your church supports.
4. Call a friend and work together on a school or youth group project.
5. Run an errand for a neighbor.
6. Volunteer to help out at an inner-city mission or homeless shelter.
7. Help a classmate in a subject in which you excel.

Loneliness Busters

1. Organize a series of games for the children in your neighborhood.
2. Visit a convalescent home or retirement community and talk with some of the residents.
3. Put together a care package for a missionary overseas whom your church supports.
4. Call a friend and work together on a school or youth group project.
5. Run an errand for a neighbor.
6. Volunteer to help out at an inner-city mission or homeless shelter.
7. Help a classmate in a subject in which you excel.

Loneliness Busters

1. Organize a series of games for the children in your neighborhood.
2. Visit a convalescent home or retirement community and talk with some of the residents.
3. Put together a care package for a missionary overseas whom your church supports.
4. Call a friend and work together on a school or youth group project.
5. Run an errand for a neighbor.
6. Volunteer to help out at an inner-city mission or homeless shelter.
7. Help a classmate in a subject in which you excel.

TWO

Outta Fright!

KEY CONCEPT: Confronting fear

BIBLE PASSAGES: Psalm 27:1-14; Isaiah 43:1-5

OBJECTIVE: As a result of this meeting, students will know how to confront fear in their lives.

MATERIALS CHECKLIST:

- ☐ Bibles
- ☐ Pens or pencils
- ☐ Candy
- ☐ Poster board with chart (or chalkboard or erasable-marker board)

Active Bonus

- ☐ Copies of "Phascinating Phobias"

JUNIOR HIGH/MIDDLE SCHOOL ADAPTATION: There is no question that early adolescents experience fear, so this topic and meeting will be quite relevant to them. Just be sure to speak at their level, using words that they understand and discussing specific fears and what students can do about them. Instead of "Film Fears," have kids share scary stories that they have heard at camp. Later, instead of breaking into groups of three to five read and discuss the verses one at a time as a group.

STARTERS

(20 minutes)

Film Fears

Have students name the source of fear related to these movies (the answers are in parentheses). Toss a "Starburst" or other piece of candy to each student who gives a correct answer.

Friday the 13th (Jason)
Jaws (the shark)
Halloween (Michael Myers)
Nightmare on Elm Street (Freddie Krueger)
101 Dalmatians (Cruella DeVil)
Psycho (Norman Bates)
Wizard of Oz (Wicked Witch of the West)
Arachnophobia (Spiders)

Fears through the Ages

Draw a chart on poster board, or the chalkboard, and have students list the fears that they had, have now, and expect to have in these different stages of life:

0 - 3 years *4 - 9 years* *10 - 16 years* *17 - 25 years* *26+*

STUDY

(15 minutes)

Discussion

Discuss the sources of fear in our society. Ask how they compare with fears in Jesus' day. (You may need to remind them that life in the first century differed greatly from today. Jesus lived in a land ruled and occupied by foreign soldiers, and long before antibiotics or other advanced medicines. People had little protection against drought and other threats to the food supply. And they also had no guns.)

Then discuss the problems of fears—how do fears hurt us? (They can keep us from taking actions we should; they can make us do irrational things; etc.)

Bible

Say something like: **Fear has been with us since Adam and Eve left the Garden and had to worry about their tomorrow. Fear of the unknown, the future, failure, and death have always been around. As with everything in Scripture, what the Bible says about fear is as relevant today as it was in Jesus' day. Let's look at some of those passages.**

Break into groups of three to five and have them discuss these passages. They should look for the fear in the specific passage (if it's mentioned), what the Bible says about it, and how to deal with it.

- 2 Corinthians 7:5-6 (People can calm our fears.)
- Isaiah 43:1-5 (Fear of threats to our safety; God protects those He redeems.)
- Psalm 118:6 (Fear of others; we should not fear people because God is with us.)
- Psalm 27:1-14 (Fear of others; we should be courageous and wait for God's deliverance.)
- Proverbs 3:21, 24 (Wisdom brings peace of mind.)
- John 14:27 (Jesus has left us with His peace; therefore, we should trust in Him.)

Have each group give a summary of what they learned about God from what they read.

CHALLENGE

(7 minutes)

Talk To

Say something like: **We have seen that fear is a universal emotion—everyone is afraid at some time or another. Some fears are irrational; in other words, they aren't based on fact. For example, someone might be afraid of darkness or water or monsters under the bed. Other fears are very justified. Whatever the source of our fears, they are real to us.**

Our fears also change as we grow older. When you were a little child, your biggest fear might have been of the dark or of being left alone by your mother or father. Right now you may be fearing for your future or be anxious about a relationship, your classes, or a performance. Your parents' fears are different, aren't they? Think of what their concerns are. They might have fears about health, *your* future, financial security, and so forth.

The problem with fear is that it can cripple us. Some people are captive to their fears—paralyzed with fright. So it is important to learn how to face our fears and deal with them.

After seeing what the Bible says about fear, it should be obvious that God will help us overcome it. I'm not saying that it will be easy, but God has promised victory over fear. One way is to practice God's presence when we are afraid. We can do that by remembering or re-reading the passages that assure us of His presence and strength. Think of how these verses can calm your fears.

Read the following passages aloud:

- Psalm 23:1-4
- Matthew 6:33-34
- Psalm 56:3-4

Ask students how the truth in each passage can help them deal with their fears. (Psalm 23:1-4—Take comfort in God; Matthew 6:33-34—Focus on furthering God's kingdom; Psalm 56:3-4—Trust in God.)

ACTION

(3 minutes)

Prayer

Pause for silent prayer. Encourage kids to talk to God about their fears and to thank Him for His presence.

Explain that you and others will be available to talk to anyone who has a special need. Then encourage students to identify the sources of fear in their lives this week (for example: movies, TV shows, music, new situations, etc.), to read over some of the passages you looked at together, and then to pray, offering their fears to the Lord.

ACTIVE BONUS

Phascinating Phobias

Hand out this list of phobias as kids enter the room. Match each of the phobias with it's proper definition. (Note: Don't laugh! These are actual, terrifying fears suffered by real people.)

1. Demophobia	a. The fear of crossing a bridge.
2. Musophobia	b. The fear of confinement in closed places.
3. Arachibutyrobphobia	c. The fear of crowds.
4. Gephyrophobia	d. The fear of peanut butter sticking to the roof of your mouth.
5. Belonephobia	e. The fear of insanity.
6. Claustrophobia	f. The fear of stairs, elevators, or escalators.
7. Astraphobia	g. The fear of public places.
8. Lyssophobia	h. The fear of lightning.
9. Hydrophobia	i. The fear of needles.
10. Climacophobia	j. The fear of mice.
11. Agoraphobia	k. The fear of water.
12. Ailurophobia	l. The fear of responsibility.
13. Hypengyophobia	m. The fear of cats.
14. Thalassophobia	n. The fear of everything.
15. Panphobia	o. The fear of the sea or ocean.

Answers: 1. c; 2. j; 3. d; 4. a; 5. i; 6. b; 7. h; 8. e; 9. k; 10. f; 11. g; 12. m; 13. l; 14. o; 15. n

THREE

The Age of Rage

KEY CONCEPT:

Controlling Anger

BIBLE PASSAGES:

Proverbs 15:1; 29:11; Ephesians 4:26-27

OBJECTIVE:

As a result of this meeting, students will understand how to deal with their anger in healthy, God-honoring ways.

MATERIALS CHECKLIST:

- ☐ Bibles
- ☐ Pens or pencils
- ☐ "Agree" sign
- ☐ "Disagree" sign
- ☐ Bible study sheets
- ☐ Copies of the "Anger Meter" worksheet

Active Bonus

- ☐ A chalkboard and chalk, or erasable-marker board and markers

JUNIOR HIGH/MIDDLE SCHOOL ADAPTATION:

Do early adolescents get angry? You bet your middle school they do! They will be able to identify with this topic. Use the meeting as written with the following changes. Use "Fireworks" right after "Fake Anger" (see Active Bonus) instead of "Agree and Disagree." And in the "Bible Search," make sure the small groups are supervised.

STARTERS

(10 minutes)

Fake Anger

Have a student secretly prepared at the beginning for what you are about to do. During announcements and/or your welcome time, this student should rudely talk aloud to his or her neighbors. You should ask the student several times to stop talking. Eventually, pretend to lose your temper: storm over, yell, and yank the student out of his or her chair. As you shove the student out of the room, give a ridiculous punishment. Then walk back to the front and announce the topic: anger. It may take a moment for everyone to realize that the outburst was a setup.

Agree and Disagree

Have two signs on the wall at the front of the room (or on opposite walls with a large group) that read "Agree" and "Disagree." Instruct your students to stand by the appropriate sign as you read off each of the following statements.

1. Anger is a sin.
2. People who lose their temper are immature.
3. It's healthier to explode and express your anger than to seethe quietly for a long time.
4. "I have the right to be angry with someone who hurts me."
5. "Don't get mad, get even."
6. Time heals all wounds and ultimately resolves the problem of anger.

Afterward, comment on the consensus or lack of it in the group.

STUDY

(20 minutes)

Bible Search

Break into small groups or pairs. Have students look up the following verses and discuss the accompanying questions. Write the verses and questions on the board or print out the verses and questions on sheets of paper.

ONE

Ephesians 4:26-27
Mark 3:1-5

- What does Ephesians 4:26-27 say about anger? (We will feel angry at times, but we can control ourselves so that anger doesn't cause us to sin.)
- Is anger good or bad? How can you be sure? (Anger itself isn't good or bad. Jesus felt angry toward sin. What makes anger positive or negative is how we act upon it.)
- What does it mean not to allow the sun to go down on your anger? (To deal with it right away.)
- What does it mean that Jesus felt anger? (Anger can be an appropriate response to evil or sin.)

TWO

James 1:19-20

- What kind of life does anger produce? (An unrighteous life.)
- What is the secret of being "slow to become angry"? (Talk less; listen more; wait before responding in a flash of anger.)
- How do you square this passage with the fact that Jesus got angry? (Jesus did not live in a state of constant anger, nor did He let anger control Him. He sometimes felt angry and responded with control. He was slow to become angry, and so should we.)

THREE

Genesis 4:3-8
Proverbs 29:11
Proverbs 29:22

- According to these verses, what can anger cause us to do? (It can cause us to lose control and do evil things we would not normally do.)
- When have you seen anger affect someone's life in a negative way?

FOUR

Proverbs 15:1; Proverbs 17:14
Proverbs 19:11
Proverbs 22:24-25

- According to these verses, what are some practical ways to stop anger in our lives before it even gets started? (Be patient; overlook offenses; don't make friends with hot-tempered people.)
- When have you seen these principles work in real life?

Bring the group back together and briefly discuss their findings and thoughts. Summarize by pointing out that anger is a normal part of being human. If we let it control us, we will sin—perhaps worse than we thought possible. If we learn to be patient, forgiving, and self-controlled, we will avoid big mistakes and create peace.

CHALLENGE

(5 minutes)

Talk To

Say something like: **Anger is our natural reaction when someone wrongs us, or when we *think* someone has wronged us. As our study showed, it's *not* a sin to get angry. The Lord Jesus himself got angry at injustice and sin. You must understand that we *can* be angry *without* dipping into sin!**

When we lash out at others, we often do enormous damage. On the other hand, when we suppress our angry feelings, we

risk becoming bitter and depressed. Someone has wisely said: "Anger is the powerful acid that can do damage to the vessel in which it is stored as well as the object on which it is poured."

So how should we handle anger? What should we do with feelings of rage?

We have just looked at a number of practical Scriptures. Let's have some of you share what you discovered. What wise advice do you have for each other?

Allow time for a number of kids to share.

ACTION

(10 minutes)

Have students spend five minutes filling out the "Anger Meter" worksheet.

After kids fill out the "Anger Meter" worksheets, in small groups have each student share which of these situations would produce the most anger in his or her life and why. Encourage other group members to offer advice and practical counsel on how to respond less angrily to each situation.

ACTIVE BONUS

Fireworks!

Do this right after "Fake Anger."

Have students reach into a jar and pull out a scenario to act out. All the scenarios deal with volatile situations:

- Parents telling a kid he/she can't go out with friends, without giving a reason.
- Turning on the TV to find your favorite show is being preempted by reruns of "Hee Haw."
- Being tripped and spilling your tray in the cafeteria in front of 400 other people.
- Getting tons of homework the weekend of a big dance.
- Not being chosen for the team when the coach's no-talent kid made it.
- Discovering that your new car got scratched.
- Getting grounded for finishing a fight that a sibling started.

ADDITIONAL IDEAS

1. Have students enter the room and write on brown butcher paper how they would complete this statement: What ticks me off most is. . .

2. Play a game of charades, or "Win, Lose, or Draw" in which one team is given ridiculously easy clues and the other is given very difficult clues. This will surely spark anger and cries of "unfair!" and will serve as a natural lead-in to the "Agree and Disagree" game.

Easy Clues	*Hard Clues*
Heart	The Kremlin
Shoe	Devotion
Cross	Salvation
Stairs	Motorcycle policeman
Giraffe	Rhesus monkey

Anger Meter

Rate your level of anger in each of the following situations:

	Minor Irritation		Slow Burn		Hot Under Collar		Steaming Mad		Volcanic Eruption!	
	1	2	3	4	5	6	7	8	9	10

- You catch your sweetheart with someone else.
- Your parents ground you for six weeks.
- A sibling borrows and breaks your stereo.
- A fellow student loses your notebook crammed with important notes.
- A teacher embarrasses you in front of the whole class.
- A friend is killed by a drunk driver.
- Your complexion goes berserk the day before a big date.
- Someone steals your wallet or purse during gym class.
- You find out a friend has been lying to you and about you.
- You get a ticket for going 41 in a 30 mph zone.

FOUR

The Not-So-Great Depression

KEY CONCEPT:	Overcoming depression
BIBLE PASSAGES:	2 Corinthians 1:8-11; 12:7-10
OBJECTIVE:	As a result of this meeting, students will know how to combat depression.
MATERIALS CHECKLIST:	☐ Bibles ☐ Tape or CD player ☐ Tape or CD of your choice ☐ Overhead projector or erasable-marker board ☐ Copies of the "Getting Down" worksheet *Active Bonus* ☐ Pens or pencils ☐ Copies of the "Depression Test"
JUNIOR HIGH/MIDDLE SCHOOL ADAPTATION:	Early adolescents are very susceptible to depression because they are growing and changing so rapidly. Often their emotions are like a roller coaster, up and down with stomach-churning frequency. This meeting should work well as written. Just be sure that in Action the scenarios involve junior-high students. Then discuss the scenarios as a group, not in small groups.

STARTER

(10 minutes)

Musical Introductions

To begin the meeting, tell kids that as the music plays, they should shake hands and introduce themselves to as many people as possible. When the music stops, they should pair off with the person whose hand they are still holding (or whose hand they just dropped or whose hand they were about to grab) and take turns asking each other the following questions. (Write the questions on an erasable-marker board or an overhead transparency projecting on the front wall.)

- **What is your favorite class at school and why?**
- **Who has had the biggest influence on your life and why?**

Then play the music again and have everyone continue shaking hands. This time, when it stops, they should grab a partner and ask each other these questions:

- **If you could eat lunch with two famous people, with whom would you want to eat and why?**
- **What is one thing that gets you sad or even depressed?**

Play the music one final time. This time, when it stops, they should ask these questions of each other:

- **What causes depression?**
- **What counsel would you give a friend who complained of being depressed?**

STUDY

(20 minutes)

Bible Study

Have everyone sit down; then say something like this: **According to recent projections and surveys by health professionals, one half of all the people in this country from the ages of 15 to 50 will battle depression at some point in their lives. Did you catch that? *One half!* That's a *huge* number. It means that some of us may be battling the blues right now. It also means that some of us probably know someone who is feeling down in the dumps.**

What can we do when those feelings of depression overtake us? Is there any hope? Do we just have to sit and wait for things to get better? Or can we take action to combat depression?

I want us to spend the next few minutes looking at some Bible verses on this topic. Believe it or not, the Scriptures have a lot to say about this very common and very ancient problem.

Divide into groups of four and hand out the "Getting Down" worksheets. Have the groups look up the verses and answer the questions (or have everyone look up the verses on their own).

Afterward, bring the groups back together and discuss their findings. Here is a reproduction of the questions and some possible answers wherever appropriate.

ONE

Numbers 11:10-15
Psalm 13:1-2
Jeremiah 20:14-18

- Who is speaking in each of these passages? (Moses, David, and Jeremiah.)
- What feelings are described in each of these passages? (Depression, discouragement, despair.)

TWO

Match the Bible passages with the possible reason for the depressing feelings described.

1.	Numbers 14:1-4	a.	Trying to live for God in one's own strength
2.	Ephesians 4:26	b.	Refusing to admit and turn from sin
3.	Psalm 32:3-4	c.	Having a complaining, unthankful spirit
4.	Job 1	d.	Suffering personal loss
5.	Romans 7	e.	Holding in one's anger

The answers to the matching exercise are: 1. c; 2. e; 3.b; 4.d; 5.a

THREE

- Which of these "causes" of depression do you think is most common? (See what teens say.)
- Which of these depression-causing actions, if any, best describe your situation right now?

2 Corinthians 1:8-11
2 Corinthians 12:7-10

- According to these verses, how can depressing circumstances bring good results? (They can teach us to rely on God.)
- How did the Apostle Paul look at depressing situations in life? (As teachers; as opportunities to trust God and to see Him work miracles.)

CHALLENGE

(5 minutes)

Assignment

Have kids brainstorm *practical* ways to overcome depression. List these on the marker board or overhead transparency. You may need to prime the pump by giving suggestions of your own. You will definitely want to note (if the kids don't mention them) some of the simple actions that Christian health professionals have found help chase away the blues . . . activities such as prayer, trusting in Christ for salvation (a great chance here to explain the Gospel and talk about the hope Christ brings), sharing feelings with a friend, laughing, exercising, praising and thanking God, and, especially, helping others.

Illustration

When students have listed a number of responses, close with this illustration about the healing that helping brings:

Dr. Karl Menninger, a famous psychiatrist, once gave a lecture on mental health and was answering questions from the audience.

"What would you advise a person to do," asked one, "if that person felt a nervous breakdown coming on?"

Most people expected him to reply: "Consult a psychiatrist." To their astonishment he replied: "Lock up your house, go across the railway tracks, find someone in need, and do something to help that person."

Then say: **That is absolutely true! Directing our focus *outside* ourselves works wonders in changing the feelings we have *inside* us.**

ACTION

(10 minutes)

Have your kids play the role of counselors. In small groups or pairs, have them read and discuss the following scenarios (one per group). Have them say what questions they would ask, what counsel they would give, and what treatment they would prescribe.

1. Joann is a high-school sophomore and friend who is acting extremely strange. Upon questioning, she bursts into tears and rambles on about how worthless she is and about how "I just wish I could die."
2. Jack tells you he can't sleep and feels restless and is unable to concentrate on his studies. "What's wrong with me?" he asks.
3. Charmaine announces, "I'm fat and ugly and need something to pick up my spirits. Come with me to the mall and help me pick out some new clothes."
4. Breck's mom died a month ago after a lengthy illness. You notice that he is withdrawing and is no longer outgoing and friendly. On Friday night you invite Breck to go see a new comedy movie with you; his response is, "No, I think I'm just gonna stay home and listen to some CD's."
5. Barb has been feeling down in the dumps for some time now. She finally says to you, "I keep praying and asking God to help me feel better—more 'up'—but it seems like God is a million miles away."

Prayer

Close in prayer. Encourage kids to focus their prayers on the good things in their lives for which they are thankful.

ACTIVE BONUS

As an alternative to the "Musical Introductions" starter, you may wish to give your students the following Depression Test to begin the meeting. (Or you could insert it after a shortened version of "Musical Introductions.") The answers are: 1. Y; 2. Y; 3. N; 4. Y; 5. N; 6. N; 7. Y; 8. Y; 9. N; 10. Probably "Y," though there is no right answer.

Depression Test

	Yes	No	
1.			Difficulty sleeping, loss of appetite, and feelings of restlessness may be symptoms of depression.
2.			Twice as many females as males experience depression.
3.			Depression is a sin.
4.			Severe depression requires medical attention.
5.			By reading the Bible and being a good Christian, a person can guarantee that he or she will never get depressed.
6.			There is little a person can do to overcome feelings of depression.
7.			Severe depression, if not treated, can cause a person to attempt suicide.
8.			A poor diet, lack of exercise, and extreme stress can cause feelings of depression.
9.			Seeing a counselor is only necessary in extreme cases of depression.
10.			I know someone who I would consider depressed.

Getting Down

Look up the verses and answer the questions:

ONE

Numbers 11:10-15
Psalm 13:1-2
Jeremiah 20:14-18

Who is speaking in each of these passages?

What feelings are described in each of these passages?

TWO

Match the Bible passages with the possible reason for the depressing feelings described.

1. Numbers 14:1-4	a. Trying to live for God in one's own strength
2. Ephesians 4:26	b. Refusing to admit and turn from sin
3. Psalm 32:3-4	c. Having a complaining, unthankful spirit
4. Job 1	d. Suffering personal loss
5. Romans 7	e. Holding in one's anger

Which of these "causes" of depression do you think is most common?

Which of these depression-causing actions, if any, best describe your situation right now?

THREE

2 Corinthians 1:8-11
2 Corinthians 12:7-10

According to these verses, how can depressing circumstances bring good results?

How did the apostle Paul look at depressing situations in life?

CHURCH

FIVE

Body Language

KEY CONCEPT:	Why go to church?
BIBLE PASSAGES:	Hebrews 10:19-25
OBJECTIVE:	As a result of this meeting, students will be able to explain their personal reasons for involvement in church.
MATERIALS CHECKLIST:	☐ Bibles ☐ Pens or pencils ☐ Poster board or banner paper and markers ☐ Old hymnals ☐ Index cards ☐ Paper ☐ Two offering plates *Active Bonus* ☐ Copies of the "Church Trivia Quiz"
JUNIOR HIGH/MIDDLE SCHOOL ADAPTATION:	Since many young people stop going to church altogether during their junior-high years, this lesson comes at a good time for them. Use it as written except in the Study section; instead of having them answer the questions, talk through the lessons of Hebrews 10:19-25 with the group. Also, when you "Pass the Plate," be ready to suggest a number of ways that junior highers can become involved in church (by greeting newcomers, taking the offering, working in the nursery, etc.).

STARTERS

(10 minutes)

Church Is

Get a big piece of blank poster board or banner paper. Across the top of it write, "Church is . . ." Hang the paper on a wall. As kids enter the room, have them write their own definitions.

Hymn Drill

Divide into teams. Pass out an old set of hymnals so that there is at least one hymnal for every other team member. Explain that you will call out a description of something from a hymn in the book. Whoever finds the hymn first wins 1,000 points for his or her team. Note: A hymn can be used only once. Ask for the following:

- A hymn with the word "love" in it
- A hymn written by someone named Wesley
- A hymn with words about an attribute of God
- A hymn with the word "blood" in it
- A hymn with an unusual word (such as "Ebenezer")
- "Amazing Grace"
- The hymn on page 27 (not necessarily hymn number 27)
- A hymn in 6/8 time
- A hymn about heaven
- A hymn with a chorus
- The last hymn in the book
- (Add others)

Determine the winning team.

STUDY

(25 minutes)

Excuses

Ask the group what kids at school think about going to church. Then ask what kinds of reasons people give for not going. Have someone write these reasons on the board.

Read the following typical statements people make about church:

- **"It's full of hypocrites."**
- **"I can worship God better alone, out under the trees."**
- **"Why should I have to sit and listen to someone tell me what they think God has said to me?"**
- **"I find it easier to believe things that someone hasn't told me I have to believe."**

Ask students how they would answer each statement. Discuss this briefly. Make sure you have thought through your own answers.

Have students look up Hebrews 10:19-25. In the NIV translation these verses include five commands that begin with "Let us." Ask students to identify the commands and explain each one:

- Let us draw near to God. (verse 22)
- Let us hold unswervingly to the hope we profess. (verse 23)
- Let us consider how we may spur one another on toward love and good deeds. (verse 24)
- Let us not give up meeting together. (verse 25)
- Let us encourage one another. (verse 25)

Ask them to explain whether the writer was thinking of Christians doing these things alone or together. (Answer: together)

Ask: **Which do you think would be the greater motivation for making church a regular part of someone's life: (a) Because they were convinced they needed what they could find at church? or (b) Because they were convinced they were needed by others at church?**

Pass the Plate

Use a couple of offering plates for this. Distribute two index cards and a pencil to each person. On one card have each person write one thing that he or she really needs from church. Then pass the plate to collect all the cards. Next, have each person write one thing that he or she has to offer the church. Pass the plate and collect the cards.

Read the first stack of cards aloud. See if there are patterns or any unusual statements. Comment on how those needs can be met in church.

Then read the second stack of cards. Add other ways that your kids can make solid contributions to the life of the church.

CHALLENGE

(5 minutes)

Use the following outline as a challenge and share your personal reasons for church participation. Explain that when people say they have no need for church, it's usually for one of these reasons:

1. They feel guilty.
2. They are unconcerned about their spiritual life.
3. They are coming off a painful experience or a disappointment with church.
4. They are ignorant of the possibilities in church.
5. They think that church has nothing to offer.

Explain that if they know Christ as Savior, they probably won't have reasons 4 and 5. Then talk briefly about 1, 2, and 3, and encourage students to become involved to make church what it should be.

ACTION

(5 minutes)

Have students choose a way that they can become more involved in church. Close by asking them to pray for people they know who are isolated or insulated from church right now.

ACTIVE BONUS

Church Trivia Quiz/Race

Divide into teams. Give each team the following questions that you have answered ahead of time. They must find the answers as quickly as possible and return to the meeting. Impose a five-minute time limit.

1. How many pews or chairs are in the sanctuary?
2. How many windows are in the east wall of the sanctuary?
3. What color is the carpet on the stage?
4. How many chairs or pews are in the choir loft?
5. How many black keys are on the piano keyboard?
6. What is written on the church cornerstone?
7. What was the cover of last week's bulletin?
8. How many cribs are in the nursery?
9. Roughly how many people can sit comfortably in a pew in our church?
10. What brand is the pastor's microphone?
11. What color are the pew Bibles?
12. What brand is the church organ?

ADDITIONAL IDEAS

Heavy Letters

Have your kids play the part of an apostle and write a letter to their church. Tell them to keep it brief (no more than one page), and to use one of the New Testament epistles as a pattern. Their letters may contain any or all of the following:

- A greeting
- Words of praise for the audience
- Instruction about how to solve a problem
- Words of challenge
- Words of rebuke
- Encouragement

Why Go to Church?

If you feel your students would benefit from being able to answer the question, "Why go to church?" have them look up these passages after you read the "typical statements" in Study.

To worship God

Psalm 95:6—"Come, let us bow down in worship, let us kneel before the Lord our maker."

To get to know God better

Colossians 1:10—"And we pray this in order that you may live a life worthy of the Lord and may please him in every way: bearing fruit in every good work, growing in the knowledge of God."

To find out how God says we need to live

Acts 2:42—"They devoted themselves to the apostles' teaching and to the fellowship, to the breaking of bread and to prayer."

To fellowship with other believers

Hebrews 10:24-25—"And let us consider how we may spur one another on toward love and good deeds. Let us not give up meeting together, as some are in the habit of doing, but let us encourage one another—and all the more as you see the Day approaching."

To become better equipped to minister to others

Ephesians 4:11-13—"It was he who gave some to be apostles, some to be prophets, some to be evangelists, and some to be pastors and teachers, to prepare God's people for works of service, so that the body of Christ may be built up until we all reach unity in the faith and in the knowledge of the Son of God and become mature, attaining to the whole measure of the fullness of Christ."

To use spiritual gifts to serve the family of God

Galatians 5:13—"You, my brothers, were called to be free. But do not use your freedom to indulge the sinful nature; rather, serve one another in love."

1 Peter 4:10—"Each one should use whatever gift he has received to serve others, faithfully administering God's grace in its various forms."

SIX

Anticipation!

KEY CONCEPT:	Looking forward to worship
BIBLE PASSAGES:	Exodus 20:1-8; Luke 14:7-11
OBJECTIVE:	As a result of this meeting, students will understand that worship is not entertainment but participation.
MATERIALS CHECKLIST:	☐ Bibles ☐ Numbered chairs ☐ Numbered slips of paper ☐ Copies of the church descriptions in "Worship Design" (Additional Ideas)
JUNIOR HIGH/MIDDLE SCHOOL ADAPTATION:	Junior highers need to understand and appreciate worship, so this is a good topic for them. The "Impromptu Service" should work well, but keep it simple—scale it down a bit. Then, instead of discussing the conceptual side of worship, spend time teaching kids *how* to worship. In other words, teach them how to take Communion, how to listen to the sermon, how to meditate, and so forth.

STARTERS

(15 minutes)

Impromptu Service

Beforehand, prepare numbered pieces of paper with the following elements of a typical worship service on them.

Order of Worship

1.	Give the welcome
2.	Lead a song
3–4.	Take the offering
5.	Give announcements
6–13.	Sing in the choir
14.	Lead a song
15–17.	Sing in a trio
18.	Read the Scripture
19.	Give the sermon
20.	Pronounce the benediction

Note: You can involve more students by adding choir members, etc.

Beforehand, make sure that chairs are set up in rows (use folding chairs if possible), and tape the numbers under the chairs. After everyone has been seated, tell them to look under their chairs to find their numbers. Write the names next to the assignments on your "Order of Worship" sheet. Explain that you've heard that many of them have been dissatisfied with church, so right now you are going to have an impromptu worship service. Then call each person up to the front to lead his or her portion of the service. Give the song leaders the songs to lead, the choir the song to sing, and the reader the Scripture to read, but let the others create their own content.

Discussion

Ask the students the meaning of "worship" and make sure you explain how *you* plan to use the word.

Our English word *worship* simply means worth-ship; that is, to declare the worth or value of someone or something.

Worship has been defined as a total response of all that we are—thoughts, feelings, desires, and body. We don't worship God to get something for ourselves, but to praise God because He is worthy to be praised.

In one sense, worship is like complimenting God for the way He is and for the things He does.

STUDY

(15 minutes)

Ask students to describe an unusual worship service in which they took part.

Then ask them to describe the most meaningful worship service they have attended.

Ask: **Is it more important to "get something out of worship" or to "put something into it"? Why? What's the difference?**

Bible Study

Have students open their Bibles to Exodus 20:1-8. Explain: **Each of the first four of the 10 commandments has something to do with worship. What does the first commandment say and how should it affect worship?**

20:1-3	God is rescuer and will not accept less than first place in our lives.
20:4-6	No one and no thing is to be allowed equal status with God.
20:7	Even God's name is worthy of honor.
20:8	God ought to be honored by the way we live our weekly schedule.

Worship is what God deserves from us!

Continue: **But is it possible to stay up late on Saturday and wander in to church sleepy-eyed just as the service starts . . . and worship? Is worship something that happens *around* us or something we *do*?** Discuss briefly.

Have students look up Luke 14:7-11. Ask someone to read Jesus' words aloud. Then ask:

- **When Jesus shows up at the party given in His honor at your church each Sunday, do you think He follows His own advice? (Does He assume the place of humility or the place of honor?)**
- **If Jesus were describing our church service, how would we fit into His description—are we the hosts or fellow guests?**
- **What would be the "lowest place" in our church?**

CHALLENGE

(5 minutes)

Talk To

Say: **Imagine that Jesus shows up here every single Sunday. He's never sick, tired, late, bored, or absent. He slips in and humbly takes the place that no one else would want. He waits for us to recognize Him, to think about Him, to welcome Him, and say to Him in prayer, "Jesus, you take the best seat in the house—I want to worship you!" What would happen in our service if so many people prayed that way that Jesus suddenly allowed us to see Him?** Discuss briefly.

ACTION

(5 minutes)

Invite students to become part of the 7–11 group (Luke 14:7-11)—a group that decides that they will make sure to "welcome Jesus" each time they meet for a worship service. Allow them to respond, then designate several to remind the group in some way to "7–11" each Sunday.

ACTIVE BONUS

Use the following suggestions for some worship experiences with the group.

Ideas for Worship

- Get a hymnbook, a book of choruses, or a personal tape player and some praise tapes. Go some place quiet and sing softly to God, thinking about the words of each song.
- Read the Psalms out loud to God, making them your own prayers.
- Take a walk around the block and tell God what you appreciate about His creation.
- Write a letter to God, listing all the things you are thankful for.
- Write a song in which you praise God for some aspect of His character.
- Remind yourself of ways that God has helped you or shown His faithfulness to you in the past.
- Without telling anyone, offer something valuable—your time, a sum of money, a precious possession—to God.

ADDITIONAL IDEAS

Worship Design

Break into small groups (5–10 in each) and give each group one of the following church descriptions. Tell them to design a meaningful worship service for the church—not the specifics but the general elements and resources. Here are the descriptions:

- A church of 1,000 members—tends to feel large and impersonal;
- A new church meeting in a school auditorium—members tend to feel lost in the room;
- A "dead" congregation—most have grown up in church and are bored;
- An "underground" church in China—they must meet in secret and avoid being detected;
- A blind or deaf congregation;
- A very poor congregation—they have no professional ministers and few resources;
- A church with a language barrier.

Then discuss how they chose which elements to use and why, and how they overcame their barriers to true worship.

SEVEN

Church Search

KEY CONCEPT: Choosing or finding a church

BIBLE PASSAGES: Ephesians 4:1-16

OBJECTIVE: As a result of this meeting, students will know three key questions to ask in choosing a local church.

MATERIALS CHECKLIST:

- ☐ Bibles
- ☐ Pens or pencils
- ☐ Note paper
- ☐ Copies of the "Quiz-A-Rama" worksheet

Active Bonus

- ☐ Hymnbooks
- ☐ Supermarket advertising flyers

JUNIOR HIGH/MIDDLE SCHOOL ADAPTATION: This meeting will be helpful for junior highers, but, quite frankly, they are a few years away from its application. Most early adolescents have very little to say about *where* they go to church. The "Here Is the Church" starter will be too difficult for them to handle, so skip it. Instead, spend time discussing their answers to "Quiz-A-Rama." The rest of the meeting should work well as written.

STARTER

(5 minutes)

Here Is the Church

Divide into teams of at least 10 kids each. Remind them of the rhyme about the church that begins with the hands forming a church with a steeple and the thumbs forming the doors. The rhyme goes, "Here is the church and here is the steeple; open the doors and see all the people." Explain that their task is to create a new rhyme for the church that they will say as they act it out. For example, they could say: "Here is the church and here is the steeple. On Sunday night here's the parking lot; you can see it is full of cars . . . not!" Or, "Here is the choir singing so sweet. And here is the pastor; he's really neat. And here's the congregation, not making a peep. They're soaking it in, fast asleep."

After a few minutes, have the teams act out their rhymes for everyone else.

Hand out copies of "Quiz-A-Rama" and pencils or pens to each student. (The correct answers are: 1. F; 2. F; 3. T; 4. F; 5. F; 6. F; 7. F; 8. F; 9. T; 10. F.)

Take time to discuss and explain the correct answers. Ask students to reword each statement so it *is* correct.

STUDY

(25 minutes)

Say something like: **You probably did not personally choose this church. It was a family decision. I hope you agree that it is a good one—the church, that is. Someday, you will be on your own, maybe going off to college, or moving to another city. Part of maintaining your relationship with Christ will mean finding a new group of believers to be a part of. We want to prepare you now for the future.**

Ask: **How did your family decide to be part of this church?** Discuss briefly.

Have students look up Ephesians 4:1-16. Use the following questions for discussion.

1. **What familiar picture is Paul using to describe the church?** (Body)
2. **In thinking about the church, we want you to remember three important words connected with the body: Head, Heart, and Health. Which of these words does Paul use in the verses we just read?** (Head)
3. **What did Paul write about the Heart, Health, and Head of the body?**
   a. Heart—"truth in love" (v. 15), "humility, gentleness, patience, bearing with one another" (v. 2)
   b. Health—"built up" (v. 12), "unity" (v. 13), "grow up" (v. 15) "grows, builds itself up in love" (v. 16), etc.
   c. Head—Christ gives us each grace (vv. 7, 15)

4. What we are seeing is that in a Christian church:

a. Christ is the head.

b. How Christians act toward one another is considered the heart of the life.

c. There is personal and corporate health—things are happening!

Let's look at our own church for a moment:

- **How would a new person be able to tell that Christ is the *head* here?**
- **In what ways does our church show its *heart* to its members and to new people?**
- **What examples of *health* would a new person be able to spot pretty quickly?**

Note: You will want to avoid the tangent of kids pointing out flaws in the church. But if there are significant issues, you may decide to plan several discussions or meetings on what students in the church can actually do if they see something wrong or missing.

CHALLENGE

(3 minutes)

Say something like: **As long as you can remember the "Body" picture of the church, you should be able to remember three important questions to ask when looking for a church:**

1. **Is Jesus the head? (Check it out!)**
2. **Is knowing and obeying Christ the heart of this church?**
3. **Is there health around here?**

ACTION

(7 minutes)

Have students write notes to the pastor or church board, expressing what they appreciate most about the church. Encourage the pastor to share these notes with the congregation.

ACTIVE BONUS

Hymn Rap

Assign hymns and songs to groups of students. Explain that they are to perform a rap version of their song (if the song is short, they can write a new verse or two). Give them a few minutes to prepare, and then have each group perform. Here are some possible hymns and songs to use: "Amazing Grace"; "Onward, Christian Soldiers"; "Jesus Loves the Little Children"; "The Church's One Foundation"; "Blessed Be the Tie That Binds"; "The B-I-B-L-E".

Super Supermarket

One sign of our affluence is that most American families are able to shop in several supermarkets. Competition is stiff. If possible, bring in some sales flyers from the supermarkets.

Assign teams of students to each market in town. Make sure you have arranged adult drivers and transportation. Have each team visit their market and prepare to make a case for that market being the best place to shop. Areas to be explored: location, variety, atmosphere, music, staff, parking, values, etc. Have each team also buy part of the refreshments.

After teams present their case, discuss how similar this process was to what they would expect to do in looking for a church.

Quiz-A-Rama

	True	False	
1.			Churches were started by early Christians to keep Christianity alive.
2.			Churches should be made up of people who are trying to find God.
3.			Not every "church" is what Jesus would call a church.
4.			The main purpose of the church is to provide a wholesome climate for the community.
5.			By the New Testament definition, our youth group could be called a church.
6.			All church members are Christians.
7.			A Christian should try to get his or her most serious problems straightened out before he or she gets involved in a church.
8.			From what we can tell about churches in the New Testament, it is a good idea to separate age groups.
9.			The church building is not the same as the real church.
10.			A Christian can accomplish what a church does simply by being alone with God.

Plugging In

KEY CONCEPT:	Getting involved in church
BIBLE PASSAGES:	1 Corinthians 12:14-27; 1 Timothy 4:12
OBJECTIVE:	As a result of this meeting, students will identify at least one area for greater participation in church.
MATERIALS CHECKLIST:	☐ Bibles ☐ Pens or pencils ☐ Chalkboard and chalk, or poster board and marker ☐ Three children's puzzles (12 to 15 pieces each) ☐ Note paper ☐ Envelopes *Active Bonus* ☐ Jump rope
JUNIOR HIGH/MIDDLE SCHOOL ADAPTATION:	This meeting is very appropriate for early adolescents and should work well as written. Use junior high examples and illustrations wherever possible.

STARTERS

(15 minutes)

Joining In

Get three children's puzzles, the kind with only 12 to 15 pieces. Mix them together, then give one piece to each student as he or she arrives for the meeting. When you are ready to begin, point out the three areas in the room (where the puzzle shells are). Tell students to discover which puzzle their piece belongs to and to assemble the puzzles as quickly as possible. Give them a time limit. Unless the numbers happen to work out, none of the puzzles may actually be complete, since you may not have given out all the pieces.

With a small group (fewer than 10 kids), use only two puzzles. With a larger group (more than 35 kids), use more than three puzzles.

Waves

Form a large circle. Warm up by actually doing a wave cheer—the leader starts, bending his or her knees slowly and then standing back up. The next person to the right repeats. Then the action should pass around the circle. Try the following adaptation:

Facing in: Raise and lower hands; raise and lower one foot; lean in, then back

Circle Sit

Next, have students stand in a circle facing sideways, with everyone facing the same way. On the count of three, have everyone sit on the knees of the person behind them. This only works if everyone cooperates. Once they have succeeded, have them stand up.

STUDY

(20 minutes)

As a transition, explain that the church (as in each of the above Starters) works only when everyone contributes. Each and every person has a place, and an important part, in the bigger picture. God wants each of us to plug in.

(Option: If you did the last meeting, you may begin by reviewing last week's points and emphasizing that "Today we want to look at what your part in church is right now!")

Explain that if they are old enough to trust Jesus, they are old enough to have some part in the life of the church.

Ask someone who reads well to read aloud 1Corinthians 12:14-27, while the rest follow along. Ask individual students to be foot, ear, eye, and head. Each one is to say his or her lines on cue during the reading.

Afterward, ask: **What are the main points of Paul's illustration?**

- The church is made up of many different kinds of people.
- The value of people in the church does not come from their "jobs."

- When one part suffers, the whole body suffers.
- Each person who trusts Christ is part of Christ's body.
- Conclusion—that means you and me!

Then say: **At this time in your life you are taking on more and more personal responsibilities. You want to begin being treated as an adult. Today we will look at someone in the Bible who struggled as many of you do right now. This person wanted to be seen as an adult in church but often felt like a kid. Can you relate? The person's name is Timothy.**

This is what Paul told Timothy about his struggle. Read 1 Timothy 4:12-16 aloud. Have students look up the verses. Ask them to find every action Paul tells Timothy to do. List these actions on a chalkboard or poster board. (Answers: don't let anyone look down on you; set an example; devote yourself to preaching and teaching; do not neglect your gifts; be diligent; watch your life and doctrine; persevere.)

Ask:

- **How many of these actions could we do?**
- **What shape would these actions take in our church?**

Note: The last question is crucial for helping students find a place to plug into. Take time to discuss how it involves your students.

CHALLENGE

(3 minutes)

Say something like: **From the list on the board, choose one of these actions you can begin to practice intentionally.** Give students a few moments to think. Then invite two or three volunteers to reveal their choice and what they would like to see changed in their lives.

You may have already been doing this without really thinking. But now you will be acting on purpose.

ACTION

(7 minutes)

Hand out envelopes, cards, and pencils or pens. Tell your students to write on the cards: "Instead of letting others look down on my youthfulness, with God's help I'm going to be an example by: __________________________________. Ask them to be very specific when they finish the sentence. Tell them to put their names on the envelopes and then to put the cards in the envelopes. Be sure they write their names on the front. Then collect all the envelopes. After two months, return the envelopes and ask students to evaluate how they're doing.

Close in prayer.

ACTIVE BONUS

Jump Rope Record

Get a long rope and recruit two strong jump-rope turners. See how many people you can get into the act after the rope gets going. Start as a group or start with two or three kids and have others jump in while the rope is in motion. Use this as you would the other Starters—to illustrate the teamwork and cooperation needed in the church.

ADDITIONAL IDEAS

Statistics

Read these some time during the meeting, perhaps during the announcements:

The following is a public service announcement:

- **Do not ride in cars; they cause 20 percent of all fatal accidents.**
- **Do not stay home; 17 percent of all accidents occur in the home.**
- **Do not walk on streets or sidewalks; 14 percent of all accidents happen to pedestrians.**
- **Do not travel by air, rail, or water; 16 percent of all accidents happen on these forms of transportation.**
- **Only .001 percent of all deaths reported occur in Bible study or worship in church, and these are related to previous physical disorders. Therefore, the safest place to be at any time is at church! Come to church! It could save your life!**

MONEY & STUFF

NINE

Gotta Have Lotta Stuff

KEY CONCEPT:	The danger of materialism
BIBLE PASSAGES:	Matthew 19:24; 1 Timothy 6:5-10, 17-19
OBJECTIVE:	As a result of this meeting, students will understand that material wealth and possessions do not provide true happiness.
MATERIALS CHECKLIST:	☐ Bibles ☐ Pens or pencils ☐ Chalkboard and chalk, or poster board and marker ☐ Blank paper ☐ "I'd say that" and "I wouldn't say that" signs ☐ Copies of the "Earnings Match-up" worksheet ☐ Copies of the "Possession Confession" worksheet
JUNIOR HIGH/MIDDLE SCHOOL ADAPTATION:	Materialism is a very relevant topic for children of any age and especially for junior highers. This meeting should work well with your group, with the following changes: Use "What's in a Face?" (see Additional Ideas) instead of "Earnings Match-up"; use the information from "Earnings Match-up" as examples for your Challenge; in the Bible Study, be sure to have adult supervision for the three discussion groups.

STARTERS

(15 minutes)

Game: Earnings Match-up

Distribute copies of the "Earnings Match-up" worksheet and pencils or pens to each student. Have students match the entertainers with their income in 1988-1989.

Answers: 1. h; 2. j; 3. d; 4. l; 5. b; 6. i; 7. e; 8. a; 9. k; 10. c; 11. f; 12. g

(Source: *Forbes* magazine)

After a few minutes, give the correct answers.

I'd Say That

Place a small "I'd say that" sign on one wall and a similar "I wouldn't say that" sign on the opposite wall. Explain that you will be reading real quotes from high-school students. After each quote, your students should stand by one of the signs, or anywhere in between, to register their feelings about the quotes. After each quote, note how similar or dissimilar their feelings are. Ask various students why they stood where they did and to elaborate on the quote.

- "Money controls everything. With money, you have somebody with you at all times. You have power, you have a say in government. Friends? Sometimes that, too."
- "Sometimes you have money but you don't have happiness, so your life is an empty space."
- "Earning my own money has changed my attitude. I used to go out, and I'd be like, 'Mom, buy me this, buy me that.' But now, I say, 'Whoa—$60 for those boots! It took me 12 hours to make that.'"
- "I love money. I see a lot of poor people and everything, but if I was like that, I don't know if I could survive. It's important to me to have a lot of the good stuff. Clothes and stuff."
- "Money is everything. It feels good to have it. I want to make a lot of money. I don't know how, but I will. Whoever said money couldn't buy happiness didn't know where to shop."
- "To myself, having a lot of money is not important. But if you don't have money, most people think that you don't have a real life."

STUDY

(15 minutes)

Discussion

Get everyone seated and quiet. Then ask:

- **What possessions matter most to you?**
- **How would you react if you lost those possessions?** (Be specific with individuals.)

Bible Study

Divide students into three groups. Give each group a sheet of paper and a pen or pencil, and assign them one of the following passages. Tell the groups to write a paraphrase of the passage to read to the rest of the group.

- 1 Timothy 6:5b-10—Key idea: The desire for wealth results in unhappiness.
- 1 Timothy 6:17-19—Key idea: Money is really God's, so those who have it should be humble and generous.
- Matthew 19:24—Key idea: It's tough to be a rich Christian!

CHALLENGE

(10 minutes)

Discussion

After the groups have reported, ask: **How can people in other cultures live comfortably on yearly incomes that compare with our monthly incomes?** Some students may be convinced it is merely a cost-of-living issue. If no one comes up with an answer, suggest that our society trains us to want a lot of things we really don't need.

Ask: **In what ways do we learn to want things we don't need?** (Television, advertising, friends who have more.) Discuss this briefly.

Talk To

Explain that everything we need to know about money and material possessions can be summed up in two simple statements.

1. Realize its danger.

Refer back to 1 Timothy 6:5b-10 and Matthew 19:24. Make a list on the board of all the potential harms of money (the ones mentioned in these passages and other ideas that students have).

Explain that the key is to be *satisfied* with what we have.

2. Realize its potential.

Make another list of the positive effects of money (draw from 1 Timothy 6:17-19). Explain that the key is to be *generous* with what we have.

Review these two concepts:

Danger: Be satisfied with what you have.
Potential: Be generous with what you have.

ACTION

(5 minutes)

Possession Confession

Have students think back to their most prized possessions that they mentioned earlier. Pass out copies of the "Possession Confession" worksheet and pens or pencils. Challenge students to fill out these sheets and sign them. Make sure that the possessions are things that students can go a week without. (For example, someone's prized possession might be a car that is absolutely necessary for getting to work. Help this student think of another possession.) Be sure to ask your students about this at your next meeting.

Prayer

Ask God to help students keep these commitments and "unlearn" the materialism that they have been taught by our culture.

ACTIVE BONUS

Room Monopoly

Turn your room into a large Monopoly board, affixing prices and rents to various spots around the room. For example, the piano could be worth $500, with a rent of $50; the big chair could be worth $400, with a rent of $25; the chalkboard could be worth $200, with a rent of $10; and so forth. Also designate "squares" in between places and a jail. When kids come in, form teams and give each team a set amount of "money" to use in the game. Then play the game. When one team goes bankrupt, stop the game and count the money. The team with the most money wins.

ADDITIONAL IDEAS

What's in a Face?

Have students identify the Presidents and famous people on the following bills and coins:

Penny (Lincoln)
Nickel (Jefferson)
Dime (Roosevelt)
Quarter (Washington)
Half dollar (Kennedy)
Silver dollar (Eisenhower)
$1 bill (Washington)
$2 bill (Jefferson)
$5 bill (Lincoln)
$10 bill (Hamilton)
$20 bill (Jackson)
$50 bill (Grant)
$100 bill (Franklin)

$500 bill (McKinley)
$10,000 bill (Chase)

Francis & Madonna

Do a quick comparison of St. Francis of Assisi and Madonna (the pop star) using the following biographies.

- **Francesco Bernardone** (Francis of Assisi, 1182–1226) was the son of a rich merchant. As a young boy, he thoroughly enjoyed a life of luxury, partying, and attempting daring feats. But after a stint in jail, a serious illness, and a visit to Rome, he started looking at life from a different point of view. He learned about Jesus, who refused all the kingdoms of the world and the wealth and fame that go along with them. He learned that Jesus chose to associate with the poor and outcast.

  The simple but radical words of Jesus caused Francis to reject his father's wishes for him to become the successor of his wealth and business. In a public argument with his father, he stripped himself of his clothes and walked away from his wealth and security. He became a tramp, lived a sober life, and became a friend of nature. When he felt a call from God to "rebuild the church," he took it literally and started to rebuild old churches, brick by brick. Others soon joined him, and in 1209, the pope gave him permission to start a brotherhood with one simple rule, taken from the words of the Gospel: They were called "the brothers of Jesus."

- **Madonna Louise Veronica Ciccone** (1959–) was born in Bay City, Michigan. Her father works in an automobile factory. Her mother died of breast cancer when Madonna was six years old. Her new mother ruled with an iron and often cruel hand, feeding the rebellion growing in Madonna.

  After attending a David Bowie concert and several other outings that were not permitted, she left home at the age of 17, very much against the wishes of her father, who wanted her to study law. She started a new life among the outcasts, gays, and prostitutes of New York. For five years, she lived in poverty, singing and dancing in obscure nightclubs.

  In 1982 she recorded her first single, "Everyboy." A year later she scored her first real hit, "Holiday," and from there on her story can be read in almost any magazine.

Earnings Match-up

1. Mel Gibson	a. $43 million
2. Guns 'n' Roses	b. $55 million
3. Frank Sinatra	c. $41 million
4. Bill Cosby	d. $26 million
5. Oprah Winfrey	e. $125 million
6. U2	f. $57 million
7. Michael Jackson	g. $60 million
8. Madonna	h. $20 million
9. Johnny Carson	i. $33 million
10. Arnold Schwarzenegger	j. $24 million
11. Eddie Murphy	k. $45 million
12. Charles Schulz ("Peanuts")	l. $95 million

Possession Confession

I, ________________________, really like my ________________________
___________, but, I know I'll never find true happiness in this. As an exercise of submission to God and a reflection of His ownership of everything that I have, I will go one week without using this possession.

____

(signed) (date)

TEN

FLEX SESSIONS

The Great Divide

KEY CONCEPT: Learning how to manage money, not just spend it

BIBLE PASSAGE: Proverbs 21:20

OBJECTIVE: As a result of this meeting, students will write a plan for managing their money.

MATERIALS CHECKLIST:

- ☐ Bibles
- ☐ Pencils or pens
- ☐ Copies of the "Big Spender Quiz"
- ☐ Copies of the "Money Pit Worksheet"
- ☐ Copies of the "Personal Survey" worksheet
- ☐ Copies of the "Money Management Action Sheet" worksheet
- ☐ Background music tapes (money themes)
- ☐ Adhesive tape
- ☐ Money plan on poster board (for "Talk To" in Challenge)

Active Bonus

- ☐ Loose change and envelopes

JUNIOR HIGH/MIDDLE SCHOOL ADAPTATION: This is a very practical meeting that your junior-high students should enjoy. Use it as written except that instead of the "Money Pit," which probably will be too complicated for junior highers, use the "Treasure Hunt" (Active Bonus).

STARTERS

(15 minutes)

Big Spender Quiz

Distribute the "Big Spender Quiz" as students arrive for the meeting while playing background music about money, materialism, etc.

As you begin the meeting, review the answers and let the students tally their scores. Give the assessment of the scores.

Award points:

2 for each "A" answer
1 for each "B" answer
0 for each "C" answer

Read this to students:

0–7 **Unless you have an inheritance in your future, don't ever apply for a credit card. You need to get a grip on your wallet.**

8–14 **You are careful about what you spend, but you are better in theory than in practice. Better think twice before you spend.**

15–21 **You are discriminating and frugal. You will always have money. Don't be afraid to help others or give yourself a treat once in a while.**

Money Pit Leader's Guide

A. INCOME:

If their last name begins with: then their income is:

FIRST LETTER, LAST NAME	MONTHLY	ANNUAL
A B C D	2,000	24,000
E F G H	3,000	36,000
I J K L	4,000	48,000
M N O	5,000	60,000
P Q R	6,000	72,000
S T	7,000	84,000
U V W X Y Z	8,000	96,000

B. TAXES AND TITHE (per month)

INCOME	TAXES	TITHE	NET
2,000	500		1,500
3,000	750		2,250
4,000	1,000		3,000
5,000	1,250		3,750
6,000	1,500		4,500
7,000	1,750		5,250
8,000	2,000		6,000

Christian's Income (per month)

INCOME	TAXES	TITHE	NET
2,000	500	200	1,300
3,000	750	300	1,950
4,000	1,000	400	2,600
5,000	1,250	500	3,250
6,000	1,500	600	3,900
7,000	1,750	700	4,550
8,000	2,000	800	5,200

C. DEBTS

These people have these debts if birthdays fall in these months:
Credit Card Debt: JANUARY, JUNE, DECEMBER
School Debt: MARCH, AUGUST, OCTOBER

Christians are decided by their first name. If their first name begins with J through S, they are a Christian.

Instructions

Determine monthly income (see A). Their income is set by the first letter of their last name.

Their net income after taxes and 10 percent tithe is determined by income scale (see B). If they are a Christian (first names beginning with J through S), use the second scale (under "Christian's Income").

Debt is figured monthly (see C). Include in debt expense.

Money Pit Game

Distribute the "Money Pit Worksheets." Explain the code for determining their income and financial obligations. Tell them to balance their monthly spending with their monthly income.

Say something like: **Follow the instructions carefully, completing Column I and totaling your net income minus expenses. Use Columns II and III to rearrange your spending plans to match your income until the net balance is zero.**

Afterward, discuss briefly the difficulties they had making choices about where to spend and not spend. Ask: **How is this spending plan different from how you are handling your money right now?**

STUDY
(20 minutes)

Role Play

Select two students to depict a parent-teen discussion/argument about the teen spending 99 percent of the money he or she earns each week. The teen has a job at a fast-food restaurant bringing home $60 per week. The parent wants the teen to save. The teen wants to spend on fun and nice things right now.

Afterward, discuss the role play. Ask:

- **Who is right in this argument?**
- **Why doesn't the teen want to save?**
- **How could saving money now affect the teen's future?**

Case Study

Have the group react to this news release:

Injured athlete retires; claims he is broke

After three great seasons, a fine pro athlete was released from the team because of injury. He faces personal problems with the loss of his contract and salary. Despite making over one million dollars in his three-year career, he says he owes back taxes and will probably file for bankruptcy, while he looks for another job and recovers from his injury.

Then ask:

- **How can a young athlete spend one million dollars in three years and have nothing left for the future?**
- **What could he have done to prepare for a financially secure future?**

Personal Survey Worksheet

Ask students to fill out the "Personal Survey" worksheet to see where their money goes. They should not put their names on these sheets. Afterward, collect the sheets (no names) and tape them on walls around the room. Let everyone walk around and look at the sheets for a couple of minutes.

Get everyone seated again and ask:

- **Are we savers, spenders, or givers?**
- **Where does our money go?**
- **What amount of money will we have saved after the next two years of work?**
- **For what significant financial needs in the future should we be saving our money?**
- **What makes it difficult for you to save a portion of your money?**

CHALLENGE

(10 minutes)

Talk To

Say something like: **Most of us feel this way about money: First, we never seem to have enough of it; second, there never seems to be any left over to save when we are all done spending.**

Perhaps what I just said is the source of the problem: We spend first and then use what is left over to give to God or to save for the future. If that is how you handle your money, you are like most teenagers and adults.

We need to learn to manage our money. That means making thoughtful decisions about where it goes and learning how to resist the temptation to spend, spend, spend.

Proverbs 21:20 says: "The wise man saves for the future, but the foolish man spends whatever he gets." How many times have we felt like fools when at the end of several months of work we have no money saved? Often we can't even remember where all the money went.

Here's a simple plan for you to use as you manage your money. (Write the following example on poster board before the meeting.)

Start with your weekly income $100
Give the first 10 percent
to God (tithe) . . . . -$ 10

This is your money to manage . . . . $ 90

Put one-third in permanent
savings . . . . -$ 30
A bank account you will touch
only for an extreme family
emergency or for major
investments in the future that
will most likely increase in
value (such as a house,
education, or business).

Put one-third in a purchase
account . . . . -$ 30
A bank account that you use
to buy important items that will
lose their value (such as a car,
stereo, or vacation).

The final one-third is yours . . . . $ 30
Money to spend as you
wish this week.

Continue: **I know your first reaction is: "Thirty dollars? That's all I have to spend? I work hard for that money. Why can't I spend it all if I want to?"**

Well, you *can* spend it all. But the Bible says you would be a fool to do so. The Bible cautions us not to think just about being happy today or this week, but to make moral decisions, use our time, and handle our money with our eyes on the future.

The biggest deception for a young person earning money is that he or she can spend it all—100 percent of his or her income—for what he or she wants and needs. Can you imagine what would happen to you if your mother or father handled their income that way? You should ask them this week how much of their weekly income they get to spend on just *their* needs and wants.

The habits that you form handling your money now will be hard to break as you grow older. You may end up just like the pro athlete who finished his career broke.

The smart athletes look ahead to the days when they will not be earning money from playing sports. They hire an accountant who does just what I suggested you do. They take the major part of their paycheck and invest or save it. They give themselves a small amount of spending money each week, and when it's gone, it's gone! They stop spending!

You can find someone to help you manage your money. Your parents won't charge what an athlete has to pay an accountant. Find someone to help you set up a financial recordbook where you keep track of where your money goes.

You work hard for your money; don't let it slip away. Resist the temptation to buy everything in sight. If you discipline yourself, the Bible says you will be wise and you will have money for important investments in the future.

No matter how much or how little you earn each week, these principles will work for you. Start managing your money today.

ACTION

(5 minutes)

Action Plan Worksheet

Distribute copies of the "Money Management Action Sheet." Review the action steps with your students. Allow time for questions.

ACTIVE BONUS

Treasure Hunt

Before the meeting, hide a few dollars of loose change around the room (or around the yard if you meet outside). Hide it under books, chairs, and rugs; behind curtains, on top of lamps, in plain sight, etc.

Give each student an envelope. Explain that you have hidden the money, and that they can keep whatever they find. Explain also that you will give a special prize to the person who finds the most. The only rule is that they have to look for the money on their hands and knees.

Give the signal to begin and then watch out as they search. Some will be more aggressive than others. Some may even cheat by adding their change to their total. Use this as an example of the pull money has in our lives.

ADDITIONAL IDEAS

Invite a financial advisor or money manager who is a Christian to talk to the students. Try to keep it simple and action-oriented. Some prior planning will help.

Big Spender Quiz

1. When you go shopping, do you bring home items you never planned to buy?
  a. Never. I stick to my plan and budget.
  b. Sometimes, but I try not to get carried away.
  c. Yes. The bargains are too good to pass up.

2. When you get a cash gift from a relative for a major purchase (such as a stereo) do you:
  a. Check *Consumer Reports* to get the best deal?
  b. Find a friend who knows stereos and ask him or her to help you choose one?
  c. Walk in the store and buy whatever the salesman suggests?

3. How often do you borrow money because you have spent your whole paycheck or allowance?
  a. Never. I budget my money carefully.
  b. Once in a while.
  c. Just about every week.

4. When you need new clothes do you:
  a. Buy what you want regardless of price?
  b. Shop the discount stores?
  c. Make do with old clothes until the stores hold a sale?

5. When a new album comes out that you think you might want do you:
  a. Borrow a friend's copy and tape it?
  b. Listen to a friend's copy and then decide whether or not to buy it?
  c. Buy it right away?

6. How many items (clothes, books, sports equipment, etc.) in your possession do you wish you had never purchased?
  a. Very few.
  b. Some mistakes.
  c. I'm loaded with junk I never use or wear.

7. When you get ready to buy a car, what will be your most important consideration?
  a. Safe, fuel-efficient, practical.
  b. Used, but looks cool, with a great stereo.
  c. It should be new.

8. After you buy something, how do you normally feel?
  a. Satisfied.
  b. Some regrets or doubts.
  c. Great at first, then depressed.

9. How important are name brands and designer labels to you?
  a. Who cares?
  b. I buy them only on sale.
  c. Means top quality.

10. How important is spending money to have a good time on the weekends?
  a. I have a lot of fun at no cost.
  b. I spend a little every weekend.
  c. It takes plenty to go out with me.

Money Pit Worksheet

		I	II	III
INCOME				
Monthly Income		______	______	______
Taxes = 25% of monthly income		______	______	
Christian Tithe = 10% of monthly income		______	______	______
Net (take home pay) (A)		______	______	______
EXPENSES				
Non-optional expenses		500	500	500
1. Food	200			
2. Utilities	200			
3. Miscellaneous	100			
Debt Expense				
1. School Debt	200	______	______	______
2. Credit Cards	200			
Additional Expenses (choose one in each category)				
1. Housing Allowance				
A. 300,000 Home	3,500	______	______	______
B. 150,000 Home	1,500	______	______	______
C. 75,000 Home	800	______	______	______
D. Rent Apartment	400	______	______	______
2. Car Allowance				
A. Luxury sport	500	______	______	______
B. Mid-size family	350	______	______	______
C. Economy	150	______	______	______
3. Vacation Allowance				
A. 1/year, big	250	______	______	______
B. Yellowstone	100	______	______	______
C. Camping	50	______	______	______
4. Entertainment Allowance				
A. 2 week	400	______	______	______
B. 1 week	200	______	______	______
C. 1 month	50	______	______	______
5. Shopping Allowance				
A. Shop to drop	400	______	______	______
B. Run across buy	200	______	______	______
C. Get what need	50	______	______	______
Optional Expenses (choose one in each category)				
6. Savings				
A. 200 B. 100 C. 50		______	______	______
7. Furniture				
A. 500 B. 250 C. 100		______	______	______
8. Second Car				
A. 500 B. 350 C. 150		______	______	______
9. Swimming Pool				
A. 300 B. 100		______	______	______
10. Club Membership				
A. 200 B. 100		______	______	______
TOTAL EXPENSE (B)		______	______	______
NET INCOME LESS EXPENSES (B - A)		______	______	______

PERSONAL SURVEY—Where Does My Money Go?

Fill in the blanks with information on what you took in and what you spent, gave away, and saved over the last 30 days.

What I got:

How much I earned ________

How much I was given ________

TOTAL INCOME: ________

What I spent:

Transportation ________

Housing ________

Clothes/Toys ________

Entertainment ________

Food ________

Extras ________

What I gave away:

____

What I invested:

____

What I saved:

____

Money Management Action Sheet

		Yearly Amount Total
List Weekly Income	__________ X 52 =	__________
Give to God (10%)	__________ X 52 =	__________
Permanent Savings (30%)	__________ X 52 =	__________
Purchase Account (30%)	__________ X 52 =	__________
Spending Money (30%)	__________ X 52 =	__________

LOOK WHAT YOU CAN SAVE!

Who can help you manage your money?____________________

Where can you open a savings account?____________________

Where will you give your tithe? ____________________

Who can help you set up a Financial Records book?____________________

ELEVEN

Job Rob

KEY CONCEPT:	The dangers of students holding a job
BIBLE PASSAGES:	Ecclesiastes 2:20-23; 3:1-13; 4:8
OBJECTIVE:	As a result of this meeting, students will understand the dangers of holding a job while they are in school.

MATERIALS CHECKLIST:	☐ Bibles
	☐ Pens or pencils
	☐ Items for "Anything for a Buck" game, including dollar bills
	☐ Skit materials
	  ☐ table
	  ☐ plates
	  ☐ food
	☐ Raw hamburger
	☐ Copies of the "Job Impact" worksheet
	☐ "The Life Hop" materials:
	  ☐ box
	  ☐ books
	  ☐ trays
	  ☐ plastic cups
	  ☐ paper
	  ☐ prizes

JUNIOR HIGH/MIDDLE SCHOOL ADAPTATION:	Because most early adolescents are too young to be employed in the community, this meeting will not be very appropriate for junior highers. You could use it, however, if you do, use "Anything for a Buck" and "The Life Hop," and then discuss how they will have to work at balancing all their activities when they're in high school.

STARTERS

(10 minutes)

Game: Anything for a Buck

Explain that you will give a dollar to kids who will do anything for a buck. Then give a dollar for crazy stunts such as:

- Put shaving cream in your hair and form horns
- Pour a bucket of water over your head
- Stick a sock in your mouth
- Eat a piece of sushi
- Sing the "Brady Bunch" theme song (or "Flintstones," or "Gilligan's Island")
- Do an Elvis impersonation for 30 seconds
- Pour a cup of cold water down (inside) your own pants
- Others as the group leader creates or selects

Write each task on a separate strip of paper and put them in a container. Have each student reach in and pull out a task. Allow 30 seconds for starting their task. Move it quickly. Make sure you pay each person.

Burger Pit Skit

Choose students to act out this skit. Be sure they practice ahead of time.

One person sits at a restaurant table. The waiter takes his or her order for hamburgers. The waiter returns with the burger. The customer takes one bite and pulls a long hair out of his or her mouth. The customer sends the hamburger back to the kitchen with the waiter. The waiter returns with a new burger but with the same result.

It happens a third time. Each time the customer is more annoyed and outraged. He or she demands to see the cook. The cook emerges from the kitchen (off stage) dressed in a sleeveless shirt, carrying a raw hamburger patty that he is forming in his hands. As he argues with the customer about the food, he puts the hamburger patty under his armpit to flatten it into patty form while loudly disputing the customer's complaint.

When everyone groans or laughs, the actors should run from the stage.

STUDY

(25 minutes)

Talk To

Say something like: **Everybody wants a job! Maybe you could find a job as a waiter . . . or a cook!**

What are the top three reasons people want a job? Listen to the responses. The top three reasons are . . . #1—Money; #2—Money; #3—Money.

When you get a job, what does the money do to improve your life? (Let kids suggest ideas.)

Continue: **Many of your parents want you to work. It is a sign of growing up and taking responsibility.**

Some of your parents may not like what we are talking about tonight. I want you to think about the *dangers* of working too much at a job while you are in school. Working a job may be helpful to you or it may be negative and destructive to you.

First, I have a little game for you. It is called The Life Hop. (Ask three students to volunteer.)

The Life Hop

Have a straight course marked out with 10 pieces of paper taped to the floor 12 to 18 inches apart. The object is to hop on one foot the entire 10 paper stations. You can have three parallel courses of paper or one course which each student can do alternately. Every two papers should be marked "STOP."

Give each student a waiter's serving tray and an empty cardboard box (orange-crate size) to hold in each hand as they hop on one foot. The tray is to be held waiter-style over the head and the box gripped with one hand around the outer edge or handle.

When they stop at square #2, add two hymnal-type books to the box and a plastic cup filled with water to the tray. At square #4, add an additional two hymn books and a cup of water. Repeat at square #6. Challenge them to hop the final four squares without losing their load.

You can place a desirable prize at the #11 paper station spot. Challenge students to drop the box of books and pick up the prize from the floor while remaining on one foot, without losing the cups on the tray.

Give the contestants plenty of cheers and encouragement.

Afterward, say: **That wasn't easy because balance is hard to maintain when we accept additional weights of responsibility.**

You have a tough challenge to balance your responsibilities with school, family, friends, church, and social life when you are working a part-time or full-time job. Let's discuss how having a job could positively or negatively affect the other areas of your life.

Distribute copies of the "Job Impact Worksheet" and pencils or pens.

Write your comments about how a job might help a perso or hurt a person. Allow three to four minutes.

Ask for student comments on what they wrote on their worksheet. Possibl answers are:

Involvement in church: Could drop out (working Sundays and nights)
After-school activities: Give up opportunities to play sports or be in schoc clubs
Physical health: Could become chronically tired due to long hours
Friends: Could lose friends—no time to be with them
Family: No time for chores or meals together
Drinking/other drugs: Working kids feel adult stresses and often use drug and alcohol to fight stress and feel good quickly.
Help others: Have money to help—maybe limited time
Grades: Could drop—sleeping in classes during school days; no time fo homework
Social life/dating: Money to go places
Possessions: Money to buy
Worry/peace: More stress
Spiritual growth: No time for God through prayer, reading, serving

Talk through the worksheet emphasizing the positives and negatives of jol responsibilities. Allow ample time for student discussion.

CHALLENGE

(5 minutes)

Say: **Maybe you have never thought about the potential dan-gers of having a job while you are in school.**

Sometimes young people who work feel as though they ar in a vicious cycle. They work to make money that they use t buy a car that constantly requires more money (gas, repairs insurance) for which they must work additional time, leavin little or no time to enjoy the car.

When the young man complained to his father that despite al his hard work, his car expenses took all his money and hi work took all his free time, his father said, "Welcome t adulthood!"

Unfortunately, that's too often true. You are just recyclin money and possibly missing some important parts of thi special time of your life.

Many years ago King Solomon wrote these words abou working: (Have someone read Ecclesiastes 2:20-23 aloud.)

Then say: **Sometimes working leaves us feeling pressured and unhappy. We're handling money, but it is not making us happy.**

Immediately after this passage Solomon wrote: (Have someone read Ecclesiastes 3:1-11 aloud.)

Then say: **Solomon says: "Everything is appropriate in its own time." There is nothing wrong with a job, but a job can begin controlling and dominating your life. A job might reduce your church involvement because you will be asked to work on Sundays. Perhaps you will miss out on special opportunities in school and with your friends and family that will never be available to you again. You exchange these timely experiences for a relatively small paycheck. Solomon reminds us to take time for the important experiences in life. Working a job is not everything—even if it does provide money.**

I hope you will examine any job you take and work to maintain balance in your life. Take time for God, for your family, for your education, and for your friends and others.

ACTION

(5 minutes)

Challenge the students to examine their job schedules. What changes do they need to make to bring their life back into balance? Can they talk with their parents and their bosses about their work schedule?

ACTIVE BONUS

Never, Never Skit

Improvise a skit in which students demonstrate what a person should *never* do on a job interview. Repeat several times with different students. Let an adult be the potential boss—asking all the questions.

ADDITIONAL IDEAS

- Have a special late-night party for everyone who has a job. They must come in their working clothes.
- Visit each working student on the job and take three to four slides of them in action. Prepare a slide show for the group using all the photos with background music of "9 to 5" by Dolly Parton or "She Works Hard for the Money" by Donna Summer.

Job Impact Worksheet

How might having a job change a person's life in these areas? (Write descriptive phrases.)

	Positive Results	Negative Results
• Involvement in church		
• After-school activities		
• Physical health and rest		
• Time with friends		
• Time with family		
• Temptation to drink or use other drugs		
• Ability to help others		
• School performance (grades)		
• Social or dating life		
• Material possessions		
• Worry or personal peace		
• Spiritual growth and commitment		

Purge Splurge

KEY CONCEPT:	When we give, we are blessed with more.
BIBLE PASSAGES:	1 Kings 17:1-16; Proverbs 11:24-25; 2 Corinthians 9:6-12
OBJECTIVE:	As a result of this meeting, students will make a group commitment to a specific giving project.
MATERIALS CHECKLIST:	☐ Bibles ☐ Pens or pencils ☐ Chalkboard and chalk, or poster board and marker ☐ Pennies ☐ Copies of the "Budget Busters" worksheet for each student ☐ Copies of the "Kernels of Truth" worksheet for each student ☐ Copies of the "Group Giving Contract" for each student *Active Bonus* ☐ Copies of the "Poor on Purpose" game
JUNIOR HIGH/MIDDLE SCHOOL ADAPTATION:	Although many early adolescents have little discretionary income, they still need to learn to be generous. And the group project will be a very positive experience for them. Use the "Poor on Purpose" game (Active Bonus) in place of "Budget Busters." Also, your students will probably appreciate the suggestions in "Other Kinds of Giving" (Additional Ideas).

STARTERS

(20 minutes)

Priority Giving

Write the following list of items on a chalkboard or poster board. Ask a few students to rank them from "easiest to give away" to "hardest to give away." Ask for explanations.

- An invitation to dinner with the President
- A $5,000 savings bond that you'll have access to when you're 50
- A $20 bill
- All your meals for one day
- Front-row-seat tickets to your favorite group's concert
- Your space in your favorite class
- All your shoes except your oldest pair
- Your brother or sister

Budget Busters

Hand out copies of the "Budget Busters" worksheet to your students and have them get into groups of four to five. Read the top three paragraphs out loud and instruct each group to produce one list that all the group members can agree on.

After about 5 minutes, pull everyone back together and ask the following questions:

- **What are the positive benefits of each of the budget items?**
- **What would be the ramifications if each budget item had to be deleted due to a lack of funding?**
- **How many categories could be slashed before you would no longer have a church?**
- **What do you think about people who benefit from a church's ministry and who use its facilities regularly, but who do not support that church financially?**
- **At what age should a person begin to give money to their church and why?**
- **Which would you choose and why: To give money to your church, or to give money to a neighbor in need?**

STUDY

(10 minutes)

Setup

Make the transition to the Bible Study by asking these questions:

- **Our Bible study is going to involve someone you might consider very generous. Who do you know as a generous person?** (Get three or four names.)
- **Why does the generous person you know deserve that label?** (Discuss briefly.)

Bible Story

Have students turn to 1 Kings 17:1-16 and ask someone to read the passage aloud. Afterward, summarize the content of the story; say something like: **Elijah, who was one of God's prophets, had told the people of Israel that there would be no more rain because of their sin. And that's exactly what happened—they had a drought. Meanwhile, God sent Elijah to wait by a brook where God would send birds to feed him. Everything was great until the brook dried up as a result of the drought.**

God then sent Elijah to a poor, single mother to get food. Even though she had only enough flour and oil to make one last meal for herself and her son, she fed Elijah. As she made the food, she found that a miracle was occurring—no matter how many pancakes she made, her flour and oil never ran out. And they never did run out until much later when God allowed it to rain again.

Ask your students to turn to Proverbs 11:24-25 and to find the answer to this question:

- **What lesson can we learn from the widow?** (People who give generously are blessed with more, and those who are stingy get nothing in return.)

CHALLENGE

(10 minutes)

Kernels of Truth

Pass out copies of the "Kernels of Truth" worksheet and instruct students to fill in the blanks with words that accurately reflect the meaning of each verse. Allow students to work in pairs if they want to. After about seven minutes, ask for a few students to read each phrase.

After you've agreed on a project, pass out the "Group Giving Contract" and have students fill it out. Set a short-term goal for completion (one week to one month).

Prayer

Ask God to help you follow through with this project and to help your students examine how much they give and the reasons for giving.

ACTION

(5 minutes)

Group Giving Contract

Challenge your group to come up with a special giving project that they will accomplish together. Brainstorm a list of possible ideas. These could include:

Inexpensive

- Buy a Bible for a child who doesn't have one.
- Purchase postcards to send to visitors to your group.
- Send a toy to a missionary child from your church.

Moderate

- Buy a bag of groceries for a needy family.
- Buy a new outfit for a child in your church or neighborhood who is needy.
- Supply a single mom with a week's worth of diapers.

More Expensive

- Sponsor a hungry child in another country for one year (about $25/month).

Choose an idea that is realistic for your group based on:

- Group size
- Spending power of group members
- Commitment level or level of excitement about the project

ACTIVE BONUS

Poor on Purpose

Make copies of the "Poor on Purpose" instructions and cut them apart. Also make copies of the "Poor on Purpose" bills and cut them apart. Hand out one instruction and 10 bills to each student as he or she enters the room.

Tell them to follow the instructions on their slip of paper.

If everyone participates, students will spend as much time receiving bills as giving them away! It becomes fun to see that one can't get rid of his or her cash. When everyone gives, everyone is blessed.

Rules:

- No throwing bills away
- You can give away only one bill at a time
- No standing still; you must mix throughout the group
- You cannot refuse a bill if someone tries to give you one

ADDITIONAL IDEAS

Giving Check

Have students add up the approximate amount of money they have *spent* on themselves in the past month (entertainment, clothes, music, fast food, dates, etc.). Next, add up how much money they have *given* to God (church donations, gifts to missionaries, and contributions to Christian ministries).

Other Kinds of Giving

Have students brainstorm and choose nonmonetary giving projects. Some ideas are:

- Walk or ride your bike somewhere instead of insisting that your mom or dad drive you. (You'll be "giving" them the money they would have spent on gasoline and wear on the car, and you'll get physically fit.)
- Take those clothes you've outgrown to an inner-city mission.
- Take those Christian books you've already read and mail them to someone in prison.
- Give to missions at least half of all the money you receive unexpectedly.
- Write to a prisoner or a prisoner's kid.
- At the end of every day, begin dumping all your change into a jar. When the container is full, roll up your coins, cash them in, and give that money to a needy family or a worthy ministry.
- Send an older person stamps so he or she can write to faraway grandchildren.
- Offer to baby-sit free for an evening for a young couple that doesn't get out much.

Budget Busters

Here's the deal: At a recent church business meeting, the youth group was appointed to make all spending decisions for your church in the coming year.

Your group's first order of business is to rank, in order of importance, the following items in the annual church budget. Simply put a "1" next to the category that you feel is most deserving of funding, a "2" next to the second most important item, and so on until you get to "10."

Remember this as you rank the items in the church budget: As long as church members support the work of the church generously, every program and project will receive funding. However, if enough gifts and offerings don't come in during the next 12 months, low priority budget categories will be slashed—or cut out altogether!

____ **Buildings**—new construction and maintenance

____ **Utility Costs**—light & water bills, air conditioning & heating costs, sewerage, garbage pick-up, etc.

____ **Music Program**—equipment, instruments, copyright costs, choir robes, music, etc.

____ **Staff**—salaries for your pastor, youth pastor, and any other ministerial personnel

____ **Missions**—support for missionaries and local outreaches

____ **Benevolence Fund**—help for the poor in your own community

____ **Youth Program**—funding for trips, socials, retreats, camps, etc.

____ **Education Program**—Bible study and/or Sunday School curriculum, teacher-training

____ **Secretarial and Custodial Help**—salaries for support personnel

____ **Office Equipment and Supplies**—purchase and maintenance of computers, typewriters, copy machines, filing cabinets, desks, envelopes, postage, paper, etc.

____ **A category of your own choosing,** in place of one above: ________________

Group Giving Contract

1. The giving project we have picked to do is: ______________________________

2. The person or group we are doing this for is: ______________________________

3. Our group has voted and agreed that we will raise this much money to complete our project: ________________________

4. The amount of money I am willing to give is: ________________________

5. I am to give my contribution to the leader on this day and time: ________________

6. Other information I should remember: ____________________________________

____

I promise to carry out my commitment to donate money to our project. I understand that by signing this Contract I am giving my word of honor to carry out this commitment.

Signed: _________________________________ Date: ____________________

Witnessed by (exchange contracts with friend): ______________________________

Important: Put this Contract where you will see it every day!

Poor on Purpose

Every time you make someone smile, give him or her a bill.

Every time you get someone to say, "Yes," give him or her a bill.

Every time you see someone *give* a bill, give that person a bill.

Every time someone speaks to you, give him or her a bill.

Every time you see someone *receive* a bill, give him or her one of your bills.

Every time you make eye contact with someone, give him or her a bill.

Poor on Purpose

1	1
1	1
1	1

Kernels of Truth

2 Corinthians 9:6-12

2 Corinthians 9:6 says: ____________ a bunch, and you'll _________.

2 Corinthians 9:7 says: Make sure you give ___________.

2 Corinthians 9:8 says: God makes it possible for you to __________.

2 Corinthians 9:9 says: God cares about ______________.

2 Corinthians 9:10-11 says: If you desire to give, God will ________________.

2 Corinthians 9:12 says: Giving to ________ equals _____________ to God.

Every volume of **Flex Sessions** gives these features:

- 3 topics of 4 sessions each—one "hot" topic, one topic on a particular aspect of spiritual life, one topic covering a tough issue
- adaptations for tailoring the sessions specifically to senior high or junior high/middle school kids
- optional activities for extra-active groups
- additional ideas and resources for expanding the sessions
- clip art

Dave Veerman, **Flex Sessions** series editor, is an award-winning writer and experienced youth worker. The writers who collaborated on these resources have written and led, collectively, thousands of meetings for high school and junior high young people. These lesson come out of their experience and creativity.

Whether teachers use **Flex Sessions** just as they're written, or pick and choose from the options available, they will find that **Flex Sessions** give the resources they need for the flexibility they desire.

Here's what youth workers and leaders have to say about Flex Sessions . . .

I highly recommend ***Flex Sessions*** *to those who are tired of digging through piles of youth curriculum hoping to find a couple things that will work. This stuff is timely, topical, biblical, and remarkably adaptable.*

Bob Stromberg
Speaker and Author

One of the questions I am most often asked is, "How do I get my kids to discuss the issues?" I think I know the answer. ***Flex Sessions*** *are especially designed to help you from planning through follow up. I highly recommend it.*

Ken Davis
Speaker and Author

Other **Flex Sessions** your group will enjoy...

Friendship, Tough Times & God's Will
Success, Pride & a Sex-Crazed Society
Sex, the Future, & Prayer
Dating, Identity & Bible Study
Helping Others, Fun and Pleasure & Knowing God
Service, Stewardship & Stress (Available June 1993)
Family, Sharing the Faith & Moral Choices (Available July 1993)

Flex Sessions are available from your local Christian bookstore.

LOST IN THE CROWD

Lost in the Crowd

OUTTA
FRIGHT
CONFRONTING
FEAR

OUTTA
FRIGHT!

OUTTA
FRIGHT!

The Age of Rage

Body LANGUAGE

Body LANGUAGE

Body LANGUAGE

OUR GOD
IS AN
AWESOME
God!

ANTICIPATION
LOOKING FORWARD TO WORSHIP

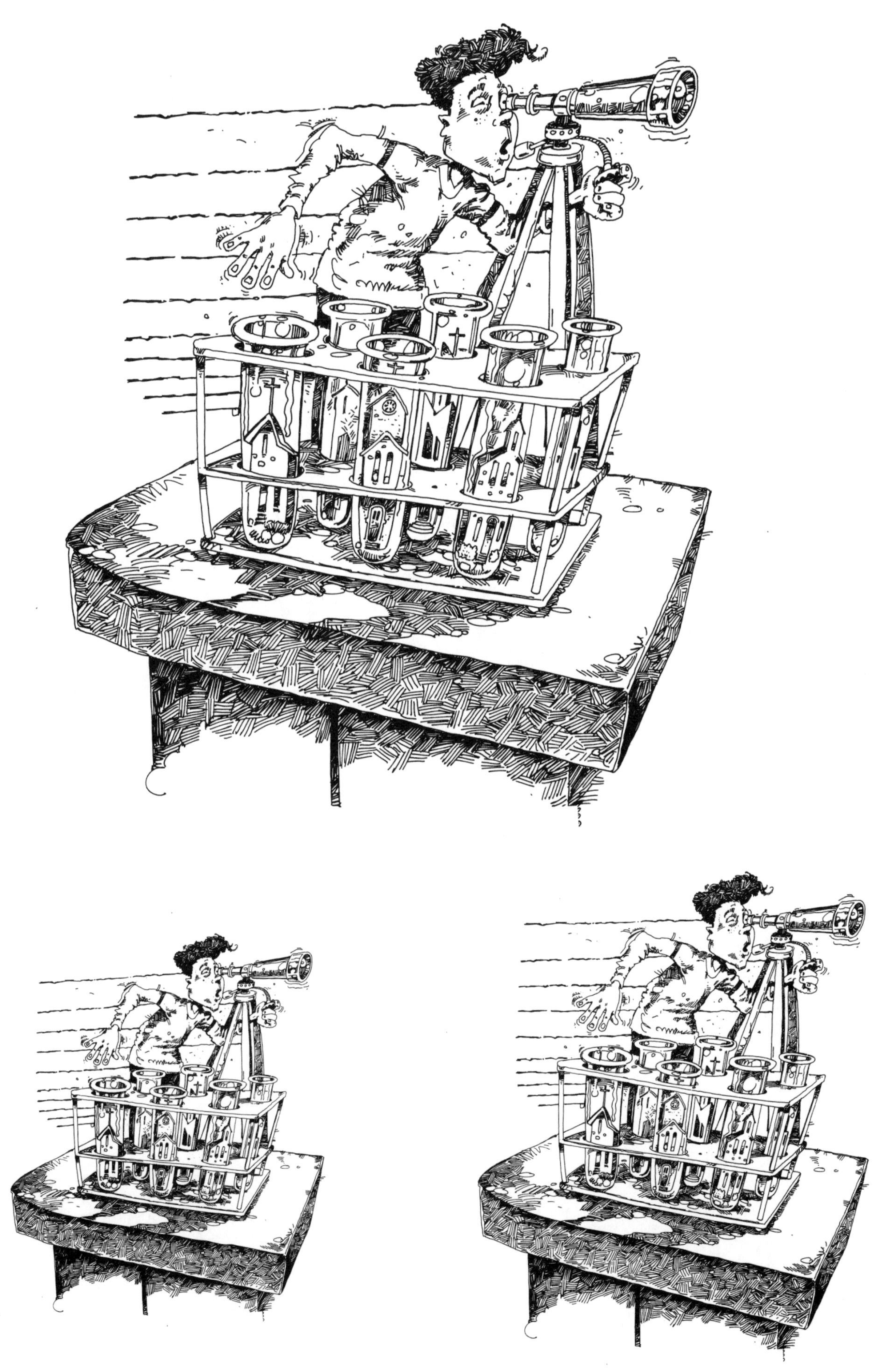

Church Search

Plugged In

GOTTA
HAVE
LOTTA
STUFF

GOTTA
HAVE
LOTTA
STUFF

MONEY PIT

THE GREAT DIVIDE

THE GREAT DIVIDE

MONEY PIT

MONEY PIT
THE GREAT DIVIDE

Job Rob

PURGE SPLURGE
GOD'S
MINE
PURGE SPLURGE
GOD'S
MINE
GOD'S
MINE